❖AMERICAN❖
RUSTIC
FURNITURE

❖AMERICAN❖ RUSTIC FURNITURE

SUSAN OSBORN

Produced by
Philip Lief & Associates, Inc.

HARMONY BOOKS
NEW YORK

Published by Harmony Books, a division of Crown Publishers, Inc.,
One Park Avenue, New York, New York 10016 and simultaneously in
Canada by General Publishing Company Limited
HARMONY and colophon are trademarks of Crown Publishers, Inc.
Manufactured in the United States of America

DESIGN: Richard Glassman, Blackbirch Graphics

Library of Congress Cataloging in Publication Data

Osborn, Susan.
American rustic furniture.
1. Country furniture —— United States. I. Title
NK   2405.083 1983   749.213   83-12823

ISBN: 0-517-55142-X

10 9 8 7 6 5 4 3 2 1
First Edition

CONTENTS

ACKNOWLEDGMENTS

We would like to thank the following people who helped prepare this book: Peter Shriver, Gene Black, Suellen Linn, Mary Fladd, Mary K. Darrah, Deanna Wish, Robert Doyle, Sally Packard, David Moore, Ken Heitz, Dan Mack, Margot Johnson, Gilbert Jaques, Harvey Kaiser, and the staff of *Fine Woodworking* magazine.

INTRODUCTION

IN SEARCH OF THE RUSTIC

This book explores the unconventional side of American furniture. To a large extent the pieces shown are the work of crafters and amateurs who have, since the earliest settlements, provided Americans with original, unassuming, and unpretentious furniture.

At its best, rustic furniture is an honest expression of the spirit of its maker. Rustic furniture is a peculiar, idiosyncratic, and cordial folk art, made for the most part by untrained artists and crafters. Influenced by diverse sources, it is often derivative but also frequently original. Although some combine shells, animal horns, hides, and other nonwood elements, most are made entirely of unhewn or unfinished parts of trees. Oftentimes the bark and moss has been carefully preserved. Some pieces made primarily of twigs have a lacelike quality and appear, in most cases, almost too delicate to withstand human use. Others, made of roots, burls, and stumps, possess a gracious and gnarled grandiosity — they are at once huge, quirky, and regal.

There is a certain inventiveness and imaginativeness in rustic furniture that is lacking in more traditional furniture. Often, the natural shape of the wood dictates the design. This is the only kind of furniture not sculpted or chiseled; parts of trees are joined as in nature; knots and disfigurations remain intact. Because rustic furniture evolved from craft traditions rather than academic traditions, the appeal of the furniture derives from the maker's unaffected and idiosyncratic design. These artisans learned by doing, and their work is typically unselfconscious. Skilled and inspired crafters, rustic furniture makers relied in the past and continue to depend today on craft techniques and their imaginations to produce honest, witty, and at times even elegant pieces of furniture.

Popular eighteenth-century design for picturesque chimney ornamentation from Ideas for Rustic Furniture, *published in London around 1785*

BACK TO NATURE

Although the use of natural material to make furniture is an age-old practice, the use of unadulterated material by crafters in the West has been sporadic. More often than not, western furniture makers have — by their sophisticated design and masterly construction — concealed the nature of the materials used.

However, during certain periods in history, artisans have struggled to restore contact with nature and the primitive sources of their art. Just such a revival of interest in the primitive occurred during the late nineteenth century, when artists and crafters — indeed all sectors of society — embraced the primitive and turned to nature as a source of moral and spiritual inspiration.

THE CALL OF THE CITY BECAME INSISTENT

The rampant urbanization that followed the Civil War affected every cultural institution, including schools, churches, and families. It altered, as well, the way urban dwellers perceived the natural world outside the city. This fin-de-siècle flight into a naive primitivism, characterized as it was by a longing for civilized if Arcadian pleasures, was expressed in songs, novels, essays, and travel books, as Americans witnessed the transformation of Thomas Jefferson's agrarian national community into a complex modern society. So wrote essayist Robert Van Court in his 1912 article "Vacation Homes in the Woods."

To those of us who live and work amid the artificiality of city life, there is something irresistibly attractive in the idea of being close to the heart of nature, wearing old clothes and living for a time the free and easy life which we like to imagine was lived before the call of the city became insistent.

THE HEALING SYMPATHY OF NATURE

It was Jefferson's belief that farmers, protected as they were from the artificiality of commerce and the city, lived lives of quiet and morally superior simplicity. They were the "chosen people of God." This dichotomy between rural good and urban evil became a popular myth, adhered to and exploited for all its worth by the cultural officiators of the nineteenth century.

Eighteenth-century designs for rustic work

The man perhaps most responsible for the nineteenth-century romanticization of nature was William Cullen Bryant. In his position as editor of the *New York Post* and spokesman for the Hudson River School, he created an ethic of Americanism that inspired artists, including Thomas Cole and Asher B. Durand, to create romantic icons of the American dream. It seems no coincidence, then, that in 1826, when Samuel Morse and Durand formed the National Academy, an institution of artists established to encourage the creation of a specifically American ethic in the arts, that Bryant was appointed "professor of mythology."

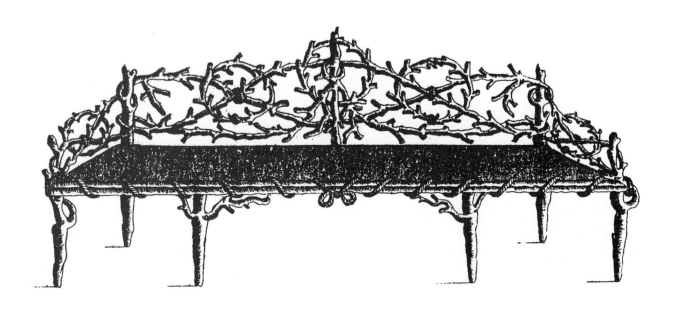

Design for rustic cottage, probably from Calvert Vaux, mid-nineteenth century

Bryant believed that nature was a crucial amenity for a moral being and was accepted by him as an alternative to traditional religion. In his *Poetical Works* he wrote, "Our own scenery has its peculiarities. . . the most striking is the absence of those tamings and softenings of cultivation. . . a farspread wildness, a look as if the new world was fresher from the hand of Him who made it. . . suggested the idea of unity and immensity, and abstracting the mind from the associations of human agency, carried it up to the idea of a mightier power and to the great mystery of the origin of things." When Bryant began referring to Cole's paintings as "acts of religion," the American forest, with its ever-metamorphosing movement and energy, became the temple for nineteenth-century America.

NATURE ENNOBLED BY REASON

When Jefferson's agrarian society found itself in the middle of the nineteenth century foundering in the floodwater of urban decadence, social historians and scientists, in search of reprieve from the false gods of the city, attempted to define the role of nature in what was becoming an obviously rabid and apparently boundless industrial society. After lengthy, if romantic rumination, it was determined that nature could, and should, be made to conform to contemporary urban tastes.

During the second half of the century, the evangelists of this back-to-nature movement were the landscape designers, who realized that by agreeing with the findings of the sociologists, psychologists, Darwinians, sexologists, and environmentalists, all of whom claimed that society could not survive without nature, a lucrative business could be had. It was then decreed: City folk must have at least occasional intercourse with peaceful, natural scenery. By the end of the century, the earnest and burgeoning middle class consulted these messianic landscape architects regularly and "country living," as cosmopolitanly experienced by the sober-minded middle class, became the highest expression of cultured society.

The first triumph of the nineteenth-century nature enthusiasts was New York City's Central Park. Designed by Frederick Law Olmsted and Calvert Vaux, Central Park stood, as Olmsted himself wrote, a "relief from the too insistently man-made surroundings of civilized life." With unparalleled grace, Olmsted and Vaux managed to transform an enormous expanse of unsympathetic terrain into something that not only imitated but tamed nature. Cultural officiators and journalists judged the value of the park by its "pastoral scenery and its restful, healing influence upon the minds of those who are worn and wearied with the strained and artificial conditions of city life." Indeed, with its extraordinary variety of trees, shrubs, and ground covers, Central Park is, in a way, superior to nature.

Inspired by Olmsted and Vaux, this desire to combine, in diverse manifestations — variation, agreeableness, and domestication — affected everyone involved in landscape design, including cemetery planners, who gradually dispensed with the morbid spruces and willows and worked — with the assistance of somewhat happier-looking plants — toward brighter, more cheerful effects.

STALKING THE PICTURESQUE

Andrew Jackson Downing (1815 — 52) is regarded by many as the premier landscape designer of the first part of the nineteenth century. He agreed with William Cullen Bryant and other cultural officiators that the city was necessary but believed that virtue could only thrive in rural settings. Being a practical sort of fellow, Downing developed a compromise plan: the now notorious suburb. By offering proximity to the city and closeness to nature, the suburb was originally devised to help people maintain better health and more moral lives.

Most of Downing's ideas on nature and design were borrowed from England. During the eighteenth century, having cast off the baroque chains imposed by the grandiloquent Louis XIV, English landscape gardeners embraced the picturesque and encouraged natural forms to meander, twist, and twirl; even the yews were allowed to go ragged. After a time, this rococo adoration of the crooked, irregular, and jagged led to the Gothic revival of the late nineteenth century.

No. 26. Spindle-back Chair. Has three arms.
Price, $2.20

Interior of cabin near Lake Placid, New York

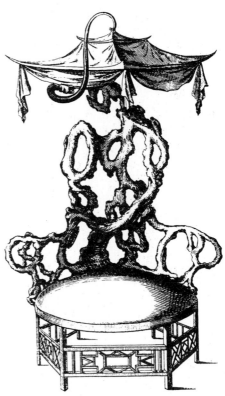

Chair design from Edwards and Darley, A New Book of Chinese Designs (London: 1754)

7

Footbridge over Ashland Creek, Lithia Park, Ashland, Oregon

Eighteenth-century design for apple-branch chair

One of the more delightful expressions of the second Gothic movement was the vine-covered cottages designed by architects for use by the beleagured middle class. It was said that within these highly ornamental and boxy structures — most of which were clasped corsetlike by all kinds of trees and shrubs — one could retreat from the dusty convolutions and ethically questionable behavior of the city and be held tight by the simple, natural, and unquestioned morality of the great earth mother. If there was a porch, it was most likely formed from the trunks of undebarked trees. Sweet-smelling creepers and delicate roses hugged the trunks and enclosed those retiring within in a delightful fragrance. Rustic chairs, often of the grotesque variety, completed the longed-for effect of total, if judiciously applied, nature.

As far as can be determined, at least three kinds of chairs appointed these porches. The first was made of gnarled, snarling roots, burly and bumpy-looking pieces that satisfied the discontented Victorians' psychological and physical need for the grotesque. Less hardy souls found themselves in rustic settees and chairs constructed somewhat more temperately of limbs and branches. And a few avant-garde homeowners bought satirical fashion pieces made of a combination of woods and styles to amuse their guests.

ROUGHING IT IN STYLE

It was during this same era that Americans, permitted for the first time the money and time for leisure, began leaving the city en masse and usually via the new railroad system in search of picturesque and rustic pleasures. Southerners traveled north from the oppressive humidity of the Carolinas and Virginia to the cooler spots in New York and Rhode Island, while northerners fled the cities for rustic summerhouses planted attractively along the more sequestered and picturesque areas of New England and, in particular, the Hudson River Valley. It was in these places, as well as in the hot-springs resorts of Arkansas, Alabama, Kentucky, and Virginia, that one found the longed-for and believed requisite tranquillity, peace, and harmony. Here one could stroll along ornamented paths, rest on seats made of logs, and feel safe, enclosed on all sides by nature's unquestionable and inexorable morality.

It was suggested — perhaps most vociferously by owners of these secluded hotels — that while in the resorts, the physical well-being of the guests was to be much benefited by regular contact with rustic furniture. Mohonk, for example, a resort in New York State, boasted not only of its sequestered setting but of its "rustic seats with straw-thatched roofs." Likewise, owners of hot-springs resorts took pains to advertise their rustic springhouses, which stood as a symbol of good health above the orifice whence purportedly sprang natural cures and longevity.

Designs for picturesque furniture from Ideas for Rustic Furniture, *published in London around 1785*

Structures in

Fig. 1.

Fig. 2.

Rustic Work

The term "rustic work" is now used for many objects made of materials, the surface or the shape of which is left in the natural condition. The smallest flower-baskets, consisting of a bowl ornamented with cones and crooked sticks, and large, even elegant, edifices, such as are seen upon our parks, are classed under the rather comprehensive name of rustic work.

Probably no finer specimens of this style of architecture can be found anywhere than at New York Central Park; the shelters, summer houses, seats, arbors, boat-landings, and bridges, built in this manner, are numerous, and are tasteful in design and executed in a workmanlike manner. It is probable that the successful introduction of rustic work at the Park has done much towards popularizing it, for we now seldom visit a neighborhood where any attention is given to rural adornment that we do not see more or less ambitious attempts at this kind of decoration and frequently excellent examples.

Work of this kind should present the expression of durability and solidity. Its very rudeness of exterior demands that there should be nothing shaky about the structure. There is no wood so well suited to the purpose as the Red Cedar, not only on account of its great durability, but because the natural growth of its branches presents a great diversity of angles and curves, twists and knots, that in the hands of a skillful workman give most pleasing effects; besides these, its color is a harmonious one. No instruction can make one a clever builder of rustic work, he must have a natural ingenuity that will allow him to combine irregular shapes into something like symmetrical forms. A mere association of grotesque branches is not pleasing. There must be an architectural design, and the details of this worked out by the ingenious use of natural materials. We give a few illustrations of simple structures. In fig. 1, we have a bird-house and a support for climbers combined. The central pillar is made sufficiently strong to support the structure, and the vines are trained to the corners by means of wires. Fig. 2 is a bridge upon the estate of Edwin A. Saxton, Esq., at Tenafly, N.J. Rustic work is often used with fine effect in small bridges, and though this is less regular in its design than some we have seen, the effect is very pleasing.

Reprinted from "The 1870 Agriculturalist"

Rustic bench, somewhere in the Adirondacks

ADVENTURES IN THE WILDERNESS:
CAMP LIFE IN THE ADIRONDACKS

It is the wild we are after . . . to the modern man in the
Adirondacks, the roar of the rapids, the gaunt dead trees around
the lake, the wet carry, the big, rotten trunks that impede his
steps, even the punkies that defy his smudge, are sources of joy
and refreshment unspeakable. He sees in them the unconscious-
ness, the spontaneity, the coarse health of the great mother
from whom we all are sprung, to whom we all return, but
whose existence we have forgotten in the cities.
 — Henry Beers, "The Modern Feeling for Nature," in *Points at Issue*
(New York: Macmillan, 1904)

The archetypical resort area developed during the latter half of the
nineteenth century was the Adirondacks, which by the 1880s and
'90s had become a mecca for urban intellectuals and benighted
nimrods alike.

The Darwinian perhaps most responsible for the taming of the
Adirondacks was the Reverend William Henry Harrison Murray,
a.k.a. "Adirondack" Murray. Murray was a man who held most
fervently, as did many clergy of the mid-nineteenth century, that
the outside of a horse was good for the inside of a man. As pastor
of Park Street Church in Boston — one of the leading temples of
evangelical Congregationalism — Murray did not hesitate to impart
his sentiment to his congregation.

It was on or about April Fool's Day, 1869, when Murray published
his *Adventures in the Wilderness*, an intense, inspirational tract that
extolled the virtues of nature. When in the woods, he wrote, "you do

*"Before and After Going into the Adirondacks."
Cartoon poking fun at the Reverend Murray's
claims about the healthfulness of life in the wilderness. From* Harper's New Monthly Magazine,
August 1870

Rustic benches, fences, and lampposts were designed to conform with the raw quality of the natural environment.

not feel like reading or talking or singing. The heart needs neither hymn nor prayer to express its emotions. Even the Bible lies at your side unlifted. You feel as if the very air was God, and you had passed into that land where written revelation is not needed; for you see the Infinite as eye to eye, and feel Him in you and above you and on all sides." One went to the woods "to have a chance to think and feel and become sanctified in an unclerical and untheological manner, that last grace of God to most men."

"The religion of the forest is emotional and poetic. No mathematician," he claimed, "was ever born amid the pines." Given the social climate of the day, it seems no surprise that within weeks of publication, there occurred a stampede to the northernmost hills of New York State, referred to as "Murray's Rush." Those in search of a new kind of sanctification, as well as cures for everything from dyspepsia to consumption, flocked to this inhospitable terrain — once even eschewed by the native Indians — in untold numbers. By July 7 of that same year, *Adventures* was in its tenth edition; to meet the demands of those who required it, the publishers put out a tourist's edition replete with a yellow waterproof cover, twelve pages of railroad timetables, and a map in the end pocket.

Of course, when the summer of '69 turned out to be cold, wet and mosquito-ridden, those participating in Murray's Rush were quickly dubbed "Murray's Fools" and Murray himself was accused of having written a "re-lieable book," one that created a situation that overtaxed the area's resources, inspired the wrong clientele, and murdered invalids.

Although hardier woodsmen protested the influx of Murray's Fools and condemned their lingering descendants — those ordinary tourists, amateur fishers, and women who had "no more taste for Nature than a rosebud has for a hurricane" — the Adirondacks did indeed blossom, and by the late nineteenth century the area had become the chic vacation spot for world-wearied and monied urbanites.

THE GREAT CAMPS

"Of everything I have experienced in America, this is probably the strangest." Thus muttered Sigmund Freud during his first look at the great camps of the Adirondacks at the turn of the century.

Built during the end of the nineteenth century, when people had money and the compulsion to spend it, the camps of the Adirondacks are unique in the history of American architecture. While "camp" literally refers to anything from a log fire in the woods to a $100,000 mansion, it was understood that these picturesque and recherché places were the summer playhouses of the rich. Here, the Webbs, the Vanderbilts, the Whitneys, and the Rockefellers fiddled with thoughts of a wild life none of them would ever dream of making permanent.

Many of the camps were designed by William West Durant (1876 – 1901) and so are similar in construction. Built by local carpenters, the camps are characterized by the use of native timber and by their harmonious integration into the surrounding area.

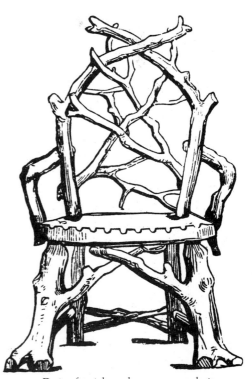

Design for eighteenth-century root chair

Original design from Old Hickory Chair Company

Sagamore Lodge, a camp now on the National Historic Register, was built in 1897 on the Blue Mountain Lake and shows characteristic Durant touches. This series of log houses made with rough bark exteriors and paneled interiors has guestrooms sufficient to hold over one hundred. As are the other camps, Sagamore Lodge is self-sufficient: The surrounding outbuildings, which include a schoolhouse, a root cellar, a greenhouse, and service buildings, are all connected by walkways.

As in the rooms of the other camps, the rooms in Sagamore Lodge were furnished with a combination of partially peeled rustic log and inlaid twig pieces, which were made on the site from the materials at hand. This rugged furniture coordinated perfectly with the rustic stairwells, lighting fixtures, chimneys, and fireplaces. Guns, fishing rods, snowshoes, animal skins, and other burly accouterments hung from the walls. Most rooms were appointed as well with an odd and often asymmetrical assortment of Japanese fans and paper lanterns. And because no guest was to be put out, every residential building was equipped with hot running water, gas illumination, and flush toilets.

THE RUSTIC REVIVAL

Although rustic furniture maintained its appeal during the early part of the twentieth century, it has only been during the past seven or eight years that there has been a forceful revival of interest in the primitive and handmade. Rustic work, considered pure in its primitivism, is being reembraced. Renowned for its moral and spiritual qualities, rustic furniture is once again enriching American homes and gardens.

Designs for rustic chairs for
summerhouses by Robert
Manwaring, The Cabinet and
Chairmaker's Real Friend
(1765)

During the last century, the moral and spiritual qualities attributed to rustic work went well beyond those derived from the construction alone: The forest was considered the cathedral God built for Himself, and some, who considered that trekking greatly promoted wholesomeness, advocated the inclusion of leisurely rambles in religious instruction.

Adirondack

Gothic

Bentwood

STYLES OF RUSTIC FURNITURE

In most of the fashionable vacation spots, rustic cottages, originally constructed to contain overflow, quickly became more popular than the main buildings. Oftentimes log structures, these cottages were dutifully appointed with rustic furniture made by country crafters. Because "settin'" was considered the most beneficial resort pastime, rockers were made in abundance, as were settees, chairs, chaises, tables, and beds.

Since the artisans were often transient and did not adhere to aesthetic regulations determined by "schools," styles vary. However, the six broad categories below offer basic if in some ways artificial diversions.

Adirondack

Because almost all Adirondack furniture was made by artisans with carpentry skills, most evinces the effect of the steel square. Constrained by the vocabulary of carpentry, these artisans were — compared to many mountain crafters — permitted little free expression, and many of the pieces demonstrate a marked inability to leave natural forms natural.

Adirondack furniture is surely the most untwiglike of all rustic furniture. These frequently heavy, often geometric, and almost excessively tidy pieces fall into three general categories. First, there are those made of split sticks, roots, and burls, applied painstakingly in a mosaiclike fashion over traditional flat-faced furniture. Twigs used to ornament these pieces were often culled from a variety of species, and the various colors and textures of the mixed woods create a uniquely dappled appearance. The second kind of Adirondack furniture is made of birch and birch bark. These pieces have been found throughout the Adirondacks, but have been located in most significant numbers in the regions around Saranac Lake and Raquette Lake. Adirondack furniture was also made of cedar. Much of the Adirondack furniture found today combines features of these three categories.

Gothic

Gothic rustic furniture usually dates from 1820 to 1850 and is, of course, now considered antique. Most of the pieces show a European influence and emphasize the irregular and grotesque: Forks, burls, roots, and other natural deformities are highlighted. Often, Gothic rustic furniture was made of the nearly indestructible rhododendron.

Bentwood

Bentwood, which experienced its heyday from 1880 to 1940, is today considered the most popular kind of rustic furniture. Usually made in the mountains and especially in Appalachia, it is romantic and free form, especially when compared to the strict geometry of the carpenter-built Adirondack. The tension of the bent pieces holds and shapes the pieces; as in Celtic art, the lines bend back on themselves, forming a pattern of amazing and logical intricacy. Many of these pieces, particularly the chairs, show an uncanny similarity to those made by Michael Thonet during the 1840s in Vienna. Michael

Thonet was a German furniture maker (1796 – 1871), who during the earlier half of the nineteenth century developed the first veneered bentwood.

Western

Closer in appearance to the carpenter-built Adirondack than the lyrical Appalachian, western-style rustic furniture is usually made of poles and slabs on the ranches of Wyoming, Montana, Texas, and other parts of the West. This rugged, indomitable-looking furniture is often made with rawhide seats and backs and is frequently ornamented with steer horns, tanned skins, and fur.

Gypsy

In general, Gypsy furniture is hastily and poorly constructed. Gypsies, not known for their appreciation of Anglo business practices, were frequently run out of town; time, therefore, was of the essence, and little attention was paid to detail. Gypsies are responsible, however, for introducing certain types of tripod tables and willow furniture. While some pieces found today are of certain Gypsy origin, because the same styles were made by Seminoles and crafters, one can never be sure just who copied whom. It is certain, though, that being transients, Gypsies spread various styles all over the country.

Factory-Made

By the 1890s, hotel and resort owners began buying thousands of pieces from factories in Indiana that produced rustic furniture. Although there were a number of factories making this furniture at the turn of the century, the first and most significant was the Old Hickory Chair Company. The factory was established by Edmund Llewellyn Brown, who upon his move from Alabama to Martinsville couldn't help but be impressed by the plethora of hickory trees in Indiana. Within months of his move, Brown was in business.

Because hickory was considered not only sturdy and upright and long-wearing furniture, Brown named his company after one of America's great and able pioneers, Andrew Jackson.

The Old Hickory Chair Company used immature hickory saplings bent into shape around a metal frame, then fitted together to make settees, tables, and chairs. While the preliminary construction was handled by men, the weaving of the backs and bottoms was completed by women and children. Every piece was marked with a brand on the rear leg or under the tabletop.

Another Indiana firm, the Rustic Hickory Furniture Company of La Porte, developed a hickory line similar to that of the Old Hickory Chair Company. These pieces can still be identified by the discreetly placed brand or paper label.

A third firm, the Indiana Hickory Furniture Company, started by a former Old Hickory employee, Emerson Laughner, may have been the only factory producing children's furniture. These pieces can still be identified by the brand on the back or leg.

Western

Gypsy

Factory-Made

PART I

RUSTIC FURNITURE: OLD AND NEW

When recommending the use of rustic furniture, Andrew Jackson Downing assured nineteenth-century homeowners that "around cottages and villa residences, nothing is so appropriate as the natural style of gardening and no ornament so proper as rustic work." Because stick furniture combines rustic charm and urban fantasy, it is as appealing to us as it was to the Victorians, and its natural and idiosyncratic character blends easily with city or country decorating schemes.

A natural, rustic living environment can be put together quickly and inexpensively. Although antiques are available through dealers and at flea markets and antique shops, they are not necessary to create a comfortable and attractive living space. Fine, reasonably priced contemporary rustic furniture and reproductions of nineteenth-century factory-made furniture provide the same feeling as antique pieces and are a quality alternative to the rare and sometimes crotchety older pieces.

The Source Guide at the end of this book includes the names of retail stores, designer showrooms, dealers, and crafters who will provide you with antiques, custom-made contemporary furniture, and factory-made pieces. Keep in mind that although most rustic furniture can be used indoors or out, some should be treated against air and moisture before being taken outdoors.

1.
CHAIRS

Popular during the 1830s and 1840s, this typical, Gothic-style root furniture shows the maker's attempt to exploit the irregularities and deformities inherent in the raw material.

Center for Music, Drama and Art, Lake Placid, New York

25

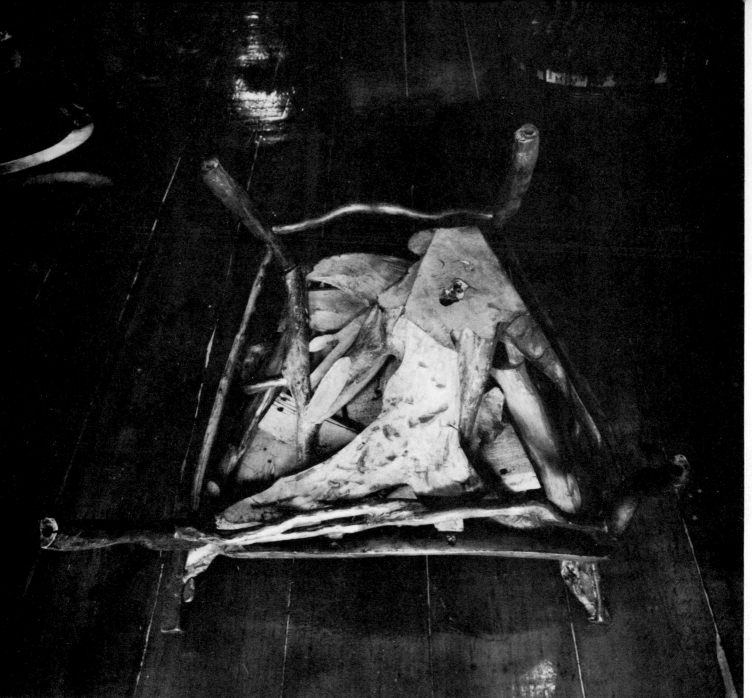

The Victorians were not the first to appreciate furniture made of twigs, branches, and other indigenous grotesque materials. During the eighteenth century, rustic furniture was an important part of the English landscape garden. The English, who had during the early years of that century been under the sway of Louis XIV (1643 – 1715), a man with a taste for the clear and measurable, embraced — upon his death — Dionysus. With the frolicsome eccentricities of the rococco came elaborate decorative schemes, a taste for chinoiserie, and probably, around 1750, the first root furniture.

George W. Gardner

The idea in making root furniture is to imitate natural growth and make the entire structure appear as if it were a living clump of woody roots. The excellent crafter who made this knobby chair during the latter half of the nineteenth century successfully imitated the asymmetrical, elemental energy of the forest. The photo on the opposite page of the chair turned upside down reveals its unique construction. Yet despite its superb deformities, this quirky little chair is comfortable to sit in. When Pie Galinat and Bob Self, foremost collectors of Americana, found this chair in Maine, it was upholstered with carpetbag material and a mouse nest. Both have been replaced.

As in early American houses in which one room was used as a sleeping, eating, and activity room, this large modern (*ca.*1950) rustic interior was designed to be a multipurpose space where a family could relax and entertain. The eclectic assortment of primitive furnishings reflects the informal atmosphere. The unusual monkey plant — *ca.*1920 — stand at the right adds just the right touch of the bizarre to this home.

George W. Gardner, at Zona Gallery

Although this contemporary armchair has a regal look reminiscent of its Victorian fore-bear, the Gothic throne chair, its clean lines and spare construction make it eminently suitable to pared-down modern interiors. While similar chairs in the West might have had seats of rawhide, Dan Mack, the New York crafter who made this piece, has used Shaker tape, one of the traditional elements of country furniture made in the East. Throne chairs make handsome pieces in the living room; they can also be used in a foyer.

During the turn of the century, when men took to the woods in droves and began telling direction by moss, they began building rustic retreats of the same dead and dry trunks and punk they hoped would provide their overwrought souls with joy and refreshment unspeakable. Made of local lumber, the rustic architecture was embellished by the use of primitive furniture made of limbs and roots. The knobby rhododendron settee below was a common decorative element. This antique piece, as well as the gnarled Gothic-style throne chair at right, add a touch of natural elegance to any setting.

Peter Lemon

Bill Beck

Each twig of the new four-shelved willow stand at the left was handpicked by Mark T. Quigley, designer and crafter of Backwoods Furniture Company in Cave Creek, Arizona. After each twig is picked, Mark pulls away the leaves and shoots, and then replants the unused branches so they will grow back in a couple of years. Once he's gathered a sufficient quantity of wood, Mark hauls his sticks back to the shop, where the straight elements are trimmed and "neatened," and the pieces required for curved supports or accents are placed in a tank to soak till they're bendable.

Although it's designed as an occasional chair, the handsome Amish oak and hickory chair below can also be used as a dining chair. Margot Johnson, of Margot Johnson, Inc., in New York, judged the age of the *ca.* 1880 Windsor-style armchair at the right by the square nails and original finish. The perfect-condition corduroy seat and brass feet make this piece especially unusual.

Amish Country Collection

"Square stones are not prisons of the body, but graves of the soul." So announced John Ruskin in 1853. Wearied by the weight of the urban life-style and square-cut stone architecture, the Victorians fled their dismal towns and raced to the gleeful ostentation of the woods. There they built vine-covered *cottages ornées* — "structures to be embosomed in trees and shrubs" — and filled them with all kinds of rustic adornment. This massive Centennial chair was made in Philadelphia in 1876 and was probably intended for use by the fireside. The poetry carved into the bark extols the traditional virtues of the rural life. Although rare, pieces such as this one are available and will help recapture an old-time feeling in any modern interior.

Left and Right: Mary K. Darrah

Factory-made or handmade, rustic furniture works. The Bangor Farmchair and Monhegan footrest below are just two of many fine cedar pieces available through Walpole Woodworkers of Massachusetts. The contoured seat and high back provide an extra bit of comfort. Likewise, the handsome contemporary dining chairs at right assure comfort as well as support. The pair is owned by caterer Garnet McKenna. Garnet says she has no system to her collecting. "I like unusual things: I see something I like and I buy it." Always an admirer of the primitive, she began collecting old and new rustic furniture seven years ago and has since recaptured the atmosphere of the eighteenth and nineteenth centuries in her apartment. The contemporary maple dining chairs blend easily with the antique pine table and recently purchased rag rug.

Walpole Woodworkers

Clarence Wheeler, an able pioneer who in all likelihood trapped his own animals, built his own cabin, and made the desk at which he sits, was not the only westerner to recognize the strength and durability of native lodgepole pine. Larry Jansen, owner of Lodgepole Furniture in Jackson, Wyoming, uses only this Rocky Mountain timber to make his "pole and slab" rockers, barstools, tables, love seats, and beds (two chairs, top right). Once they are constructed, Larry's wife, Judy, uses a single strip of rawhide to weave the seats and backs; the piece is then finished with a coat of Danish oil. Jansen, who uses only original designs,

will also custom-build. Unlike Jansen's furniture, which reveals the maker's training as a carpenter, John Coonen's furniture (left and bottom right) has a more fluid quality. Coonen, a California-based gardener and orchardist, builds furniture on rainy winter afternoons. He begins with a Y-shaped stick — the best he can find among the unculled oak trunks of the coastal hills — and then saws the branch into suitable back pieces. The seats are chopped out of first-growth redwood stumps, the headrests are black oak, and the rockers — a shape hard to find naturally in the forest — are formed of elm or birch lumber.

Photo by Joel Schopplein © 1983 The Taunton Press Inc., Box 355, Newtown, CT 06470. Reprinted with permission from *Fine Woodworking* No. 38

Photo by Joel Schopplein © 1983 The Taunton Press Inc., Box 355, Newtown, CT 06470. Reprinted with permission from *Fine Woodworking* No. 38

It's said that Andrew Jackson so appreciated the sturdy simplicity of hickory furniture that he used hickory chairs and tables to decorate the White House. While his furniture was probably constructed by the Old Hickory Furniture Company, the round-backed chair above was made by that company's heir, the Hickory Furniture Works of Indiana. As in the old days, hickory saplings are cut and dried in the winter when the sap is down, then each piece is treated for infestation, cut to length, steamed, bent, tenoned, and drilled. Every seat and chair back is woven of Tahitian slab rattan and each piece identified by a brass mark indicating the date of production and the initials of the artisan.

Most of the chairs built in the southern Appalachian mountains between 1870 and 1880 were based on Spanish contour designs, probably introduced to the area by Spanish and Portuguese Gypsies, and French basketwork chairs. The mountain crafters who made them, though, embellished the imported design with ideas of their own. The person who made the labyrinthine rocker (ca. 1880) at right emphasized the linear, energetic character of the chair by the use of multiple rods of wood; the shoots bend back on themselves in an intricate and logical pattern. The chair's restless movement is further enhanced by the chip-carved edges.

George W. Gardner, at the home of Margot Johnson

By the middle of the twentieth century, rapid technological advances provided furniture makers with a variety of newly developed materials with which to work. The use of chromed tubular steel, plywood, and plastics gained widespread application, particularly among mass-producers. However, the Amish have always stood fast against these modern "conveniences," and their furniture — elegant in its simplicity and pure in its utilitarianism — reflects the difference in their sensibility. The expert crafters who provide Amish Country Collection of Pennsylvania with chairs, tables, rockers, high chairs, cradles, and combination bookshelves/pie racks, have helped preserve some of the quiet dignity we associate with rural life.

Lewis Onson's traditional bentwood chair (*ca.*1945) was probably part of a set of eight used for "settin'" on the porch and grounds of the Pinewood Lodge.

Meticulous craftsmanship and attention to detail — that's what traditional Amish furniture is all about. Made of planed and varnished as well as unhewn hickory and oak, the two pieces shown here combine the best of rustic and finished furniture. The capacious swing at the left provides a gracious touch to any porch; the superbly designed rocker is perfect indoors or out.

Amish Country Collection

OVERLEAF:

The whimsical design of these seven-foot-tall maple ladder-back chairs (a modern design by Jon Brooks) would have appealed to the nineteenth-century avant-garde, who appreciated the satirical as well as the fashionable. Geoffrey Katz

Peter Lemon

The natural shapes of tree limbs have suggested the arms and legs of chairs and tables to furniture makers through the centuries. The contemporary love seat at right has a traditional corduroy seat and is made of unadulterated Adirondack-culled cedar. Factory-built chairs, like the antique chair (top left) and contemporary straight-back rocker (bottom right) were and still are made in Indiana, where hickory trees flourish. By far the most popular, however, is bentwood. The round-backed cypress chair below was built by Florida crafter Richard Giddens, whose father taught him the art of bending and nailing "whips" — the slim trees used for seats and backs — and "benders" — the taller trees used to shape the backs of sofas and other large pieces. The late John Giddens made thousands of pieces of twig during the 1930s and 1940s when cypress twig, rattan, and wicker were *the* Florida outdoor furniture. Cypress, which is naturally blond, will weather to a soft gray if left on the patio.

Richard Giddens

Love seat by Gilbert Jaques
Peter Lemon

Minnesota Historical Society

Hickory Furniture Works

47

Although many rustic furniture makers attribute the design of this peacock-back chair (right) to Choctaw Indians or Gypsies, self-taught Mississippi crafter David Moore suspects the design may actually be of African origin. Made of young sycamore and black willow saplings found along the banks of the Mississippi River and within the swamps that dot the small islands cluttered in the river's delta, this five-foot high, three-foot wide chair will change color with age and wear from its original blood brown to various shades of black and yellow. While nails are used to secure the different elements of this chair, in most of David's bentwood furniture the natural tension of the wood holds the pieces in place. Although the chair makes a handsome accompaniment to the contemporary and antique interiors, because it is finished with tungseed oil it will last for years in the garden.

Indiana Historical Society

George W. Gardner, at the home of the Bascove-Avramides

Always relaxed and welcoming, rustic furniture easily combines with a variety of decorating elements. The homeowners set the amiable mood of the country retreat at right with the purchase of two perfect-condition factory-built chairs. Found in New England, the chairs blend comfortably with the nineteenth-century café table and the Afghanistan dhurrie. When the pillows are removed, the chairs can be used outside on the porch or terrace.

Gilbert Jaques, the skilled artisan who built this contemporary garden seat, relies more on his imagination than carpentry techniques when making his furniture. Jaques, a retired farmer and highway superintendent, uses the cedar he finds near his Adirondack home to build the forms he sees in his head — nothing is ever drawn on paper. Interestingly, Jaques, who only began building stick furniture this year, incorporated a corduroy seat, a traditional Adirondack design element. Inside or out, this seat helps create an informal, country mood.

This standard Gypsy design is the easiest kind of rustic chair to build; in fact, New York crafter Jerry Farrell can make two or three in a day. However, unlike traditional Gypsy furniture, speed in this case does not indicate negligent construction. Farrell is a pro, his construction top-notch. Everything is made by hand, and he uses only durable ironwood. As with all rustic furniture, the natural wood tones of this armchair warm up even stark modern interiors and add a touch of country comfort.

Center for Music, Drama and Art, Lake Placid, New York

By the late nineteenth century, rustic furniture was favored by the emerging leisure class. This newly monied group read with care the words of Andrew Jackson Downing and other evangelical landscape architects and decorators who wrote of the ennobling qualities of rustic furniture: "With the decoration and improvement of his cottage and garden" with rustic furniture, Downing wrote, a homeowner's "self-respect and comfort in his home will grow." Adulated for its irreproachable character, rustic furniture was considered just the thing for formal studio portraits. By posing with this Adirondack-style birch chair, this mother silently extolled her own and her children's moral wealth.

George W. Gardner, at Zona Gallery

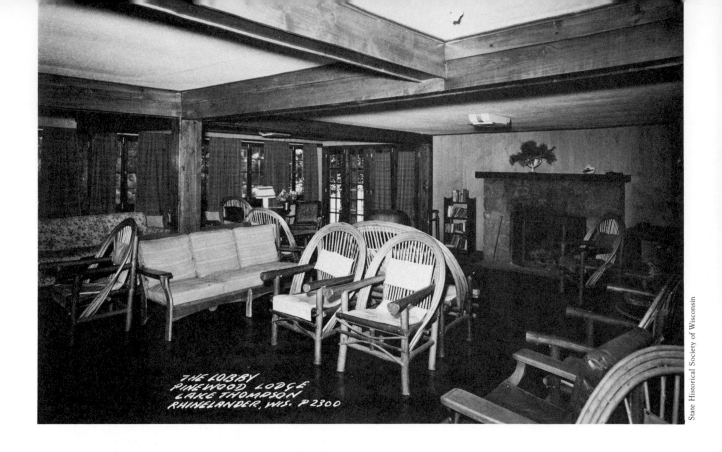

THE LOBBY
PINEWOOD LODGE
LAKE THOMPSON
RHINELANDER, WIS. P 2300

Homer Collection, Bowdoin College Museum of Art, Brunswick, Maine

Potcovers

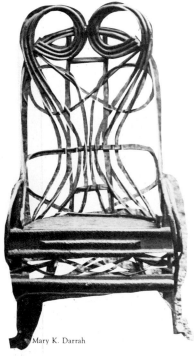

Mary K. Darrah

Some say the bentwood style was born in protest against the cabinet-maker's and carpenter's strict geometry. Unlike carpenter-built furniture, most bentwood furniture is held together not by precise joinery but rather by the tension of the bent wood. Although the bentwood style experienced its heyday between the 1870s and 1940s, this loopy and often capricious-looking furniture has been made by mountain crafters for hundreds of years. While many early crafters, hoping to cash in at the summer markets, loaded their furniture onto wagons for the trip to town, others, were content to carry their goods on mules and horses for occasional door-to-door sales. The intricate, almost Celtic design of the antique rocker on the near left is typical of rockers made in the Appalachians and other southern mountain regions. Of the pieces shown above, all but the honeysuckle basket and round Portuguese planter were made by Massachusetts crafters Rich and Tom Midwood. The brothers — who use any wood available, but predominantly willow, cherry, and birch — often combine various woods in one piece to exploit the naturally variegated colors and textures.

More like eighteenth-century root furniture than bentwood, the settee on which the bearded Winslow Homer is sitting on the opposite page was obviously made by someone with a pronounced taste for the irregular.

Many western artisans appreciated the naturally rugged shapes and forms of animal horns, hooves, and antlers and used them to make sophisticated and elegant furniture. Made of moose antlers, hooves, and leather, this antique dining set would add a touch of class to modern or "old-fashioned" interiors.

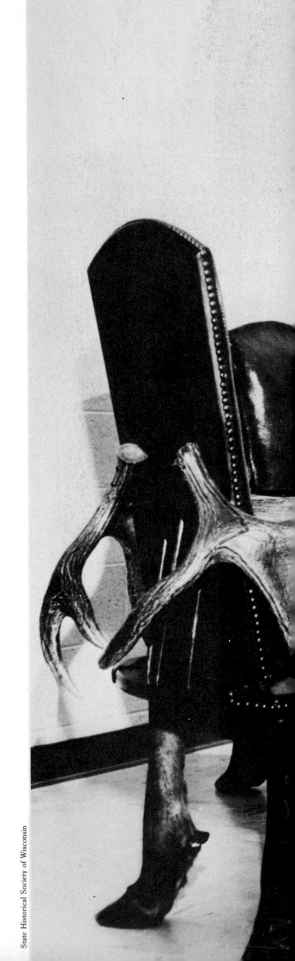

George W. Gardner, at the home of Irene Eisenberg

Although the word *rustic* is usually used to describe something with a rural character, a lot of rustic furniture, particularly those pieces made in the West, are as sophisticated and elegant as traditional furniture. The rare antique horn rocking chair and matching footstool at right were made of twenty-six matching Texas longhorns by master crafter Wenzel Friedrich in San Antonio around 1885. Both are covered with original skins and are owned by Margot Johnson, one of the country's principal collectors of Victoriana. Margot, who specializes in collecting top-quality items from the nineteenth century — including twig, wicker, Renaissance revival, Egyptian revival, and art furniture — has combined a variety of Victorian elements to create a magnificent yet comfortable living environment. Although the staghorn hatrack at left supplies a handy place for headgear, it can also stand alone as a graceful and unusual piece of sculpture.

2.
TABLES

Before air conditioning, the porch was used as a sitting room. Protected from the sun and cooled by gentle breezes, a porch or terrace still provides comfort on hot summer days. The antique, factory-built hickory furniture that complements this terrace is almost as sturdy and certainly as morally sound as it was fifty years ago. Most of the factory-made furniture was produced in Indiana from the area's plentiful hickory trees. Hickory chairs and tables, bound for the hotels of the Adirondacks, arrived by the boxcar and, despite numerous fires, are still readily available at antique shops and flea markets. Most can be identified by a trademark burned into the back of a leg or seat. Although most furniture was originally intended for outdoor use — on porches, pavilions, parks, and lawns — today's homeowners find that it works perfectly indoors or out.

Irene Eisenberg, foremost collector of rustic furniture, loves the weird and eccentric; as a result, her Tudor home is packed with an eclectic and attractive assortment of the odd and grotesque. Made of a variety of woods and adorned with a symmetrical arrangement of roots and burls, the turn-of-the-century rustic table at the left is enhanced by the playful assortment of rare knickknacks and figurines. David Holzapfel, the Vermont crafter who designed and built the nouveau Gothic cherry and birch burl table below, uses only timber — unmanageable crotches, root systems, wolf or bull butt logs, doglegs, and burls — that is of no value to the lumber industry. Made of black walnut and bass wood, the sturdy spider-legged side table at right was handcrafted by New Hampshireman Jon Brooks. Like their forebears who respected the natural and wild-grained beauty of the wood, both Brooks and Holzapfel work to bring out the natural shapes of the raw material.

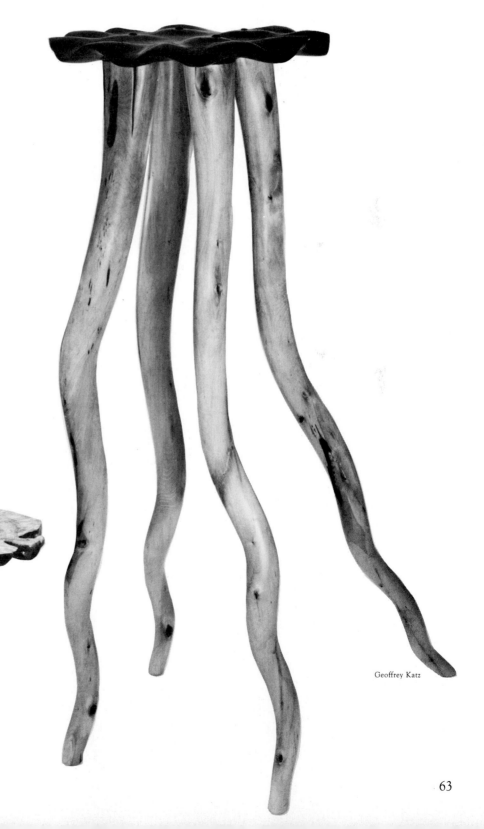

Peter Mauss

Geoffrey Katz

George W. Gardner, at the home of Irene Eisenberg

Still being made in the 1940s, the turn-of-the-century smoking stand at left features a decorated roof, an ornamented exterior, and a painted window in the front door. Although some smoking stands were mass-produced at factories, this Appalachian-style stand — the roof lifts off to reveal a compartment for one's smoking paraphernalia and the "front lawn" provides space for an ashtray — was handmade, and was probably sold from the back of the family truck as a mountain souvenir. The unhewn, antique ashtray (top right) was probably made in the Adirondacks and is set against a backdrop of prize carved walking sticks. Built in 1865, the twig gaming table below is made of 2,042 pieces of firwood and holly and is marked on the bottom with a family insignia and the initials of its maker, George W. Wood. The intricate, strictly geometrical mosaic-work top is secured completely by needlepoint; Wood used no nails or glue.

In her *Housekeeper's Manual* of 1873, the eminent domestic authority Catherine Beecher approved decorative rustic work as a "means of educating the ingenuity and the taste." Children especially, she advised, gained much in the way of competence and grace by making rustic baskets and vases. While the primitive twig planter at left demonstrates a certain elementary construction, it was probably made by a skilled Adirondack carpenter who considered woodcraft not mere child's play, but rather an essential part of his masculine image.

George W. Gardner, at Margot Johnson, Inc.

During the nineteenth century, a moral quality was attached to objects made of natural materials. Decorated with Indian arrowheads and constructed with a horn handle, the brass-and-copper ceremonial pitcher and steer-horn goblets below were probably designed with the presumed link between the religious impulse and rustic material in mind.

Although nineteenth-century aesthetes lauded things untouched and rustic, they also recognized the importance of human intervention. Keeping this in mind, and with the aid provided by countless periodicals and household manuals, professional and amateur woodworkers gathered twigs and branches and began shaping, altering, and beautifying nature. The results — as can be seen in the antique shelves at right and the rare Swiss-work table below, composed of alternating squares of wood on the top and lower shelf, with finials at the corners of the top — are as varied as their makers. The table, probably made between 1880 and 1900, is also chip-carved.

George W. Gardner, at Margot Johnson, Inc.

Now owned by Philip Lief, this baronial table may have been used at J. P. Morgan's Camp Uncas, where the cuisine was French, the goblets gold-rimmed, and the butter plates shaped of birch bark.

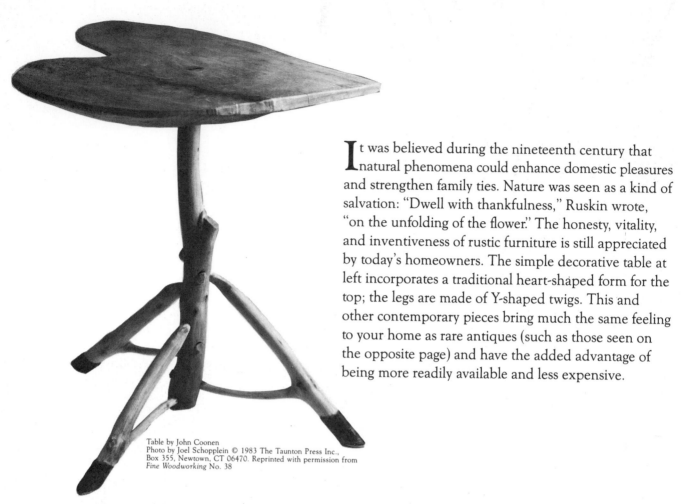

It was believed during the nineteenth century that natural phenomena could enhance domestic pleasures and strengthen family ties. Nature was seen as a kind of salvation: "Dwell with thankfulness," Ruskin wrote, "on the unfolding of the flower." The honesty, vitality, and inventiveness of rustic furniture is still appreciated by today's homeowners. The simple decorative table at left incorporates a traditional heart-shaped form for the top; the legs are made of Y-shaped twigs. This and other contemporary pieces bring much the same feeling to your home as rare antiques (such as those seen on the opposite page) and have the added advantage of being more readily available and less expensive.

Table by John Coonen
Photo by Joel Schopplein © 1983 The Taunton Press Inc., Box 355, Newtown, CT 06470. Reprinted with permission from *Fine Woodworking* No. 38

Center for Music, Drama and Art, Lake Placid, New York

Last year, when some independent Berkshire crafters realized they could not meet the growing demand for stick furniture, they joined forces, bought and renovated a hundred-and-fifty-year-old buggy-whip factory, and formed The American Rustic Furniture Company. Since then they have been providing department stores across the country with top-notch rustic furniture, like the furniture seen here. The twelve crafters who make up this old-fashioned factory use only native wood — birch, oak, mountain laurel, sugar maple, and ironwood; out of respect to tradition, blemishes and other natural deformities are left intact. Each piece is branded with the date the piece was made, and because every piece is constructed with mortise-and-tenon joints, it will last a lifetime. This elegant, literal, and affordable furniture can be used indoors or out and will add a graceful note of history to any contemporary home.

Photo by Nick De Candia at the home of Peter and Meg Stratner

Bench by Dan Mack
Photo by George W. Gardner, at Zona Gallery

The contemporary bench at left, fashioned by Dan Mack from Catskill-culled maple, typifies the Adirondack style. The strict linearity of the Adirondack carpenters contrasts sharply with the more lyrical and poetic dimensions of the Appalachian style.

The Appalachian settlers made furniture that evinces a Celtic appreciation of puzzles and intricate design. While the structure of the ornate, Appalachian-style, chip-carved table at right is essentially simple, the design is typically complex. Made during the latter part of the nineteenth century, the table was probably constructed with simple tools — perhaps a drawknife or penknife.

He who imitates nature, rigorously and faithfully, just as she is," wrote architectural theorist Francesco Milizia in 1823, "is no more than her historian, but he who composes her, exaggerates her, alters, and beautifies her is a poet." With this idea in mind and with the advice of numerous manuals and periodicals, ambitious crafters of the nineteenth century set about exaggerating, altering, and beautifying nature. These two tables are distinctive examples of the Victorians' attempt to do nature one better. By rimming the top of the spidery table at left with an even row of undebarked dentils and forming the bottom of a cluster of peeled ironwood branches, the crafter who made this piece successfully combined geometric shapes with the unique asymmetry of nature. The smaller, more symmetrical plant stand at right is no less poetic. Their simple nobility and sense of the past make them appropriate for country or urban decors.

rge W. Gardner   Tables owned by Philip Lief

George W. Gardner

3.
SOFAS & BEDS

A common folk-art motif, hearts have been used to decorate everything from boxes and sugar molds to shooting-gallery targets and banks. The folk artist who made this bedframe for Mary Ellisor Emmerling, owner of the American Country Store in New York City and author of *American Country: A Style and Source Book*, used resilient and easily shaped willow saplings for the entire construction.

In Edmund Burke's famous treatise "A Philosophical Enquiry into the Origin of Our Ideas of the Sublime and the Beautiful" (1756), he divided the visual world into two categories: beautiful objects — those that are relatively small, smooth, and regular — and things sublime — those that are huge, rugged, and of dark coloration. Although Burke's work was repeatedly cited by Andrew Jackson Downing and other evangelistic landscape architects of the nineteenth century, many criticized his disquisition on one count: There seemed to be no room for anything in the middle. Burke's failure led to the formation of a third category, the picturesque — that which has a character "not less separate and distinct than either the sublime or the beautiful," that which is pleasing to the eye and mind, rustic objects such as the nineteenth-century settees below and right.

Mary K. Darrah

George W. Gardner, at the home of Irene Eisenberg

When placed in a modern setting, old-fashioned, "clumsy" twig takes on a spare, even elegant character. This spindle-back couch was custom-built for Connecticut homeowner Dick Berry by New York crafter Ken Heitz. Ken began this piece by foraging in the woods surrounding his studio for the best-looking poplar

George W. Gardner

he could find. When finished with tungseed
oil, the smooth white poplar — the only wood
available to Ken that won't crack when peeled —
makes a clean contrast to the ruddy Mexican
terra-cotta floor. Ken, who generates his
own electricity for the few power tools he uses,
gave up a job with IBM to make twig furniture.

The rugged-looking four-poster bed above, made of two evenly split trunks, provides a brawny look to this informal bedroom. At right, a contemporary four-poster bed, similar in tone to the original Adirondack furniture, provides a similarly formidable and manly look to an airy bedroom.

Many of the original Adirondack camps were summer residences of the rich where roughing it had little meaning, but in other parts of the country, rustic camps were of a different hue. The Fin and Feather Resort of the Woods in Boulder Junction, Wisconsin, for example, has a more amiable and somewhat less pretentious character than some of the more exotic camps of New York's northern wilderness. The virile hunters and fishermen who stayed here during the thirties and forties were enclosed on all four sides by peeled logs. Guests were, however, provided with hot and cold running water and flush toilets.

Crafter Hutch Traver often ornaments his walnut and steam-bent cedar bedframes with honeysuckle vines culled from the hills around his home in North Carolina. Sophisticated yet amiable, they provide an exotic touch to any bedroom.

Peter Lemon

Simple, sturdy furniture was needed for the summer resorts that appeared in the Adirondacks at the turn of the century. Because factory-made hickory furniture such as the love seat at left was appreciated for its personality and, as one journalist for *Craftsman* magazine wrote, its "air of definite sincerity," hotel owners did not hesitate to appoint their retreats with mass-produced furniture from the factories in Indiana.

Except for the ashtrays and bottles, the bar at Johnson's Tavern and Nite Club in Webb lake, Wisconsin, is completely made of wood. During the thirties and forties, tired hunters and fishermen could refresh themselves with twenty-five-cent whiskey sours. Old-fashioneds cost a dime more.

Available through A. S. Perry, the handcrafted sofa at right looks great with pillows covered with anything from silk to chintz.

OVERLEAF:

This aristocratic bent-willow suite, handmade by Florida crafter Richard DiMarzo, may be purchased through Richard, or he will sell you step-by-step instructions if you wish to make your own.

Richard DiMarzo

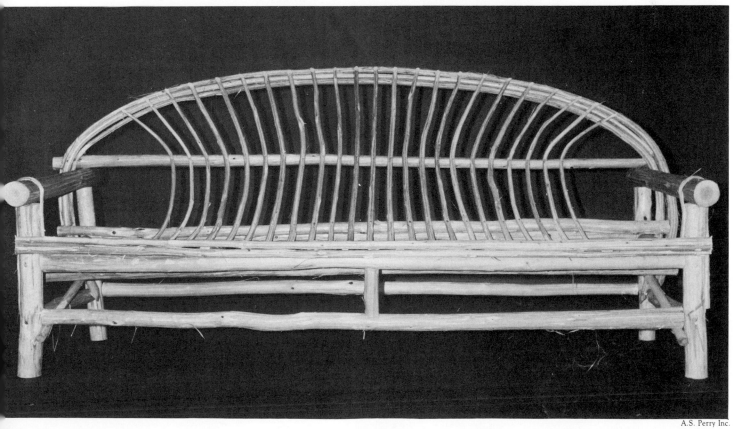

Saranac Lake Free Library

Center for Music, Drama and Art,
Lake Placid, New York

When viewing nature, the Victorians believed that the soul was conducted away from distressing scenes; one became surrounded by an atmosphere of health and tranquillity. As they were aware, the garden or yard is a natural extension of rural homes, and twig furniture perfectly accommodates itself to picturesque environments. Although the family above does not seem to have been completely transformed by nature's beneficent force, one suspects they were doing their best to feel blissful and naturally sanctified. While in all likelihood they built their own stick footbridge and sofa from wood cleared before building their camp, after the 1890s much rustic furniture, including perhaps the antique table at left, was built by factories in Indiana. Joe Callahan and Paul Myers, who bought this contemporary factory-made swing set twenty years ago, spend hot afternoons here shaded from the sun.

This pine cradle, *ca.* 1890, was probably made by a self-taught Adirondack crafter. The raggedy-toothed quilt is also from the nineteenth century.

Center for Music, Drama and Art, Lake Placid, New York

4.
RUSTIC ACCESSORIES

For many, the camps of the late nineteenth century and early twentieth stood as a relief from the "too insistently man-made surroundings of civilized life." Almost everything, including the walls of this rustic haven, is made of native birch.

George W. Gardner, at Margot Johnson, Inc.

Made of strips of birch, the roof of this rare, turn-of-the-century dollhouse lifts to reveal the original rustic furnishings, including a double-decker bed and a spinning wheel.

Rustic furniture easily co-ordinates with a variety of decorating elements, because of its natural quality. The hefty cedar-and-pine Adirondack-style hutch and hickory child's chair at left were probably shaped by a carpenter employed by wealthy camp owners, while the exemplary Appalachian-style bentwood rocker was most likely made by a southern mountain crafter. A typical Appalachian design, the well-embellished heart-motif table below is enhanced by the metal birdcage, complete with miniature rustic antlers on the front gable.

103

Nature abhors straight lines." So wrote William Kent, the influential nineteenth-century chronicler. The Victorians believed that serpentine curves and grotesque forms stimulated the imagination and soothed the spirit. Hence the velvet-covered antler chair at right. In comparison, however, to the more ornate and heavy styles of twig preferred by most Victorians, bentwood furniture is delicate and light. Willow, appreciated since Hippocrates discovered its medicinal qualities, was selected by Ohio-based crafters Debra and John Phillips for its strength and beauty. The cozy bed below is only one of over thirty pieces the Phillipses have designed since first pursuing their interest in folk art five years ago. After the design is conceived and the basic shape built, small branches are woven into the design to create an original pattern. The furniture is then nailed together and linseed oil and shellac applied. Occasionally rawhide is used to tie the pieces together. As practical as it is beautiful, willow furniture adds charm to any room of the house.

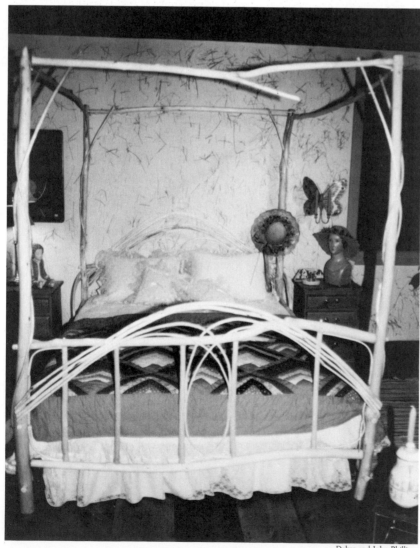

Debra and John Phillips

STAIRWAY STUZAS BIRCHWOOD LODGE G.
HAZELHURST, WIS

Although the fashion for twig furniture began in the Adirondacks, it quickly spread south and west, evolving as it traveled. The stalwart, rustic stairway of this midwestern fishing-and-hunting lodge and the wild and loopy *nouveau* Appalachian chair made by Walter Hughes of Tennessee (right) show just a few of rustic's true variations. However, whether it's in a public setting, a private office, or outdoors, it always retains its informal, unpretentious character.

Wheras urban dwellers once accessorized their homes with fine European furniture, many now accent their living rooms and bedrooms with rag rugs, shingle siding, old-fashioned dolls, and other unpretentious rustic items such as the antique child's chair, *ca.*1910, at the right. The chair is unusual because of its twisted arms and highly decorated back. The contemporary settee, armchair, and side table below are handcrafted of native North Carolina willow by a local artisan who has been making bentwood furniture since the Depression. Available through Added Oomph! of North Carolina, the furniture can be used indoors or out. During the early part of this century, John Krupsack, the dapper-looking gentleman at the left, fashioned his chair from a bush growing in his Wisconsin backyard.

George W. Gardner at Kelter-Malcé

Added Oomph!

George W. Gardner, at the home of Anthony Zunino

The Natural Light

Twigs have been used to make anything from picture frames to flowerpots and have always been an important part of country decorating schemes. The antique child's chair (above left), *ca.*1880, and the Gothic rhododendron birdcage, *ca.*1840 – 1860, help create a relaxed and informal mood. But accessories need not be old to have a country flavor. The handcrafted twig lamp (bottom right), available through The Natural Light in Oklahoma, and the contemporary child's rocker (left) have a look of the past and add a gentle touch of rusticity to modern interiors.

111

Although some objected to the Arcadian impulses of the Victorians and considered coarse cloth, football, and "worm-holed furniture" barbarizing influences, others, including the inspired maker of this elaborate gazebo, embraced the rustic and found it eminently suitable for many purposes. Sociologists and many housekeeping manualists even considered the rustic a civilizing influence on children and smog-saturated urbanites. This gazebo, with its ever-metamorphosing planes of movement and energy, imitates the magical quality of nature that was praised by landscape architects of the late nineteenth century and adulated by the burgeoning middle class.

Gothic pieces, such as the Victorian throne chair below, *ca.*1880 were often made in Europe and brought to America by emigrating families.

Mary K. Darrah

Rustic gazebos, Chinese-style footbridges, and various other kinds of garden structures were popular during the latter part of the nineteenth century and were designed to conform with the ever-changing character of the natural environment. When the call of the city became too insistent, one could collect one's soul here and enjoy the handiwork of nature. Although the relatively pared-down garden seat (above right) has a modern character to it, it was made during the last century and might very well have been found in or around these gazebos.

Center for Music, Drama and Art, Lake Placid, NY

At the turn of the century, Americans struggling to cope with the pressures of urbanization tried to define the role of nature in an industrial society. The suburbs, discrete areas that offered a proximity to the city and yet a closeness to nature, were developed, and the "country club," a place that mixed casualness with formality, emerged. Some, like this official with an Oregon forestry commission, could satiate their longings for Arcadia by working in a rustic environment. The entire structure — walls, supports, stairs, and banisters — are made of locally culled and undebarked logs and branches. The somewhat overwrought plant stand below may have been manufactured by the Niagara Falls Rustique Manufacturing Company around 1870. Rustic stands like this can be used in any room of the house to add a country atmosphere.

The Margaret Woodbury Strong Museum

PART II
RUSTIC CARPENTRY

During the latter part of the nineteenth century — it was believed that rustic furniture gave a home "an animated and interested soul," and as was frequently pointed out, by making and filling a home with rustic furniture, not only would one's home be improved and its beauty increased but one's self-respect and comfort would be likewise elevated. Today, people are embracing the rustic for much the same reasons.

Because rustic furniture does not require rigorous joinery or meticulous calculation, it can be easily constructed by anyone. When deciding on the piece you want to make, bear in mind that a great deal of the appeal of rustic furniture is derived from its irregularity and informality: The pleasure of construction comes from testing one's imagination and one's ability to improvise.

We offer the following instructions as suggestions only. The instructions have been reproduced as they appear in Paul N. Hasluck's first-rate *Rustic Carpentry*, a handbook of instructions originally published in London in 1907. As a general guidebook to the construction of rustic objects suitable for everyday use, it has yet to be surpassed. However, it cannot be emphasized too often that whatever you choose to make, it will be enhanced by a certain disregard for the measuring tools used by carpenters and traditional cabinetmakers.

Bench by Gilbert Jaques

5.
PLANS FOR BUILDING YOUR OWN FURNITURE

Rustic carpentry does not demand great skill in woodworking, but it does require a large amount of artistic perception. The tools needed are but few, and the materials employed are comparatively cheap.

For light rustic work, sticks of hazel, cherry, yew, blackthorn, birch, larch, fir, and the prunings of many varieties of shrubs may be used.[1] But it is necessary that the material should be cut at the proper season, and thoroughly dried before being worked up. The sticks should be cut in mid-winter, as at that time the sap is at rest; if cut in the summer time the bark will peel off. If peeled sticks are required, they should be cut in the spring, when the sap is rising, as at that time the rind will come off easily. In some districts the copses are cleared of undergrowth periodically, and the sticks (generally hazel) sold to hurdle and spar makers.[2] A selection of these sticks would be very suitable for the purpose here described.

The sticks should be stacked in an open shed in an upright position if possible, and in such a manner that the air can freely circulate around them. When they are required for fishing rods or walking sticks they are hung up to season — this keeps them straighter; but hanging them up is not necessary for the work about to be dealt with. When the sticks have been put away for from six to twelve months, according to size, they will be ready for use, after being rubbed with a cloth or brushed to clean off the dust and bring up the color of the bark. Fir cones may often be worked into a design, and bits of rough bark and the warts and burrs found on old elm trees may be collected by the rustic worker and put by for future use.

One method of treatment for designs in light rustic work is to split the sticks and use them to overlay the work with a Swiss pattern,[3] as shown by Fig. 1; another method is to work the sticks up after that manner that canes are used in bamboo furniture (see Fig. 15).

PHOTOGRAPH FRAME

Fig. 1 represents a wall bracket with a photograph or mirror in the frame. To make this, the piece forming the back is first cut out of ⅜ in. deal.[4] The shelf, of ¾ in. deal, is then nailed to the bottom edge. Some straight hazel, fir or other sticks are next selected and split; these are nailed round the edges of the back, and round the opening at the centre. The pieces around the opening overlap the edges about ¼ in., to form a rebate[5] for the glass. The bare spaces at the sides and top may be covered in the following manner: Take a piece of brown elm bark and run a saw into it. Catch the sawdust, and, after warming the wood, cover it with thin glue. Sprinkle the brown sawdust on the glued surface, and sufficient will adhere to cover the deal and give the frame a rustic appearance. Cork-dust or filings may be used instead of sawdust. Bunches of fir or larch cones are nailed to the corners, as illustrated; these should be pared at the back with knife or chisel to a flat surface. The outer edge of the shelf is finished with an edging of short lengths of split stick nailed on. The general construction of the bracket, and the method of fixing the glass, will be clear from Fig. 2.

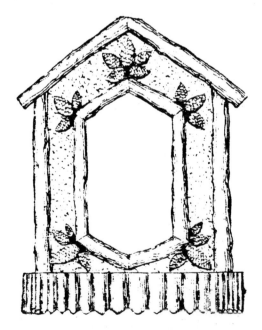

Fig. 1.
Photograph Frame and Wall Bracket Combined.

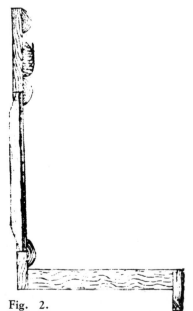

Fig. 2.
Section of Bracket, Showing Fixing of Glass.

ORNAMENTAL VASE

The rustic flower-holder for table decoration, shown by Fig. 3, consists simply of a gipsy tripod formed with six rustic sticks, put together in the form shown, and tied with a length of bass.[6] There is no attempt made at finish, but the sticks must be firmly tied together at the joints, and the ends of the bass can be left either hanging loose or tied in a bow. The holder for the flowers is a coconut shell, which has been sawn in two, so as to leave one part a sort of cup or egg shape; three holes are bored with a bradawl[7] at equal distances round the edge, and it is suspended from the tripod with three more pieces of the bass, which completes the arrangement. Of course, any small receptacle can be used in place of the coconut shell, but that, perhaps, carries out the rustic appearance the best, and is very easily obtained. Fig. 4 is an attempt to show the tripod when decorated.

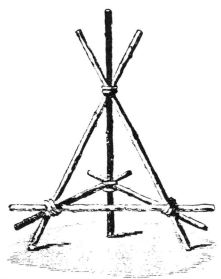

Fig. 3.
Rustic Flower Holder for Table Decoration.

Fig. 4.
Rustic Flower Holder Complete, with Coconut Vase in Position.

STOOL

The rustic stool (Figs. 5 and 6) is intended to be made in pairs, and placed one on each side of the umbrella stand above described, each supporting a plant, such as a fern or palm. The top of each stool is cut from 9 in. square 1 in. wood (wood from an old box answers well), and is sawn into an octagonal shape. A double row of pieces of apple, maple, or some other wood with good bark, is nailed around the edges, thicker pieces being used at the bottom than at the top to give a graduated appearance. The entire top is then covered with straight pieces of stick, selected for the beauty of their bark. All pieces are nailed on with brads. The four legs are formed of 1 in. apple wood 9 in. long. They are bevelled at the top to fit a square block of wood, 2 in. thick and 3 in. long, which is firmly secured

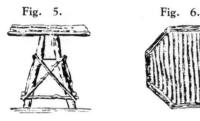

Fig. 5.   **Fig. 6.**

Figs. 5 and 6
Elevation and Plan of Plant Stool.

to the top by two screws. This piece of wood should be fastened to the top before the rustic rods are placed in position. Two 2½ in. nails through each of the legs hold them quite securely to the central block. Portions of rustic wood, from ¼ in. to ⅜ in. in diameter, are then nailed across the legs, as shown in Fig. 5, the ends being allowed to cross each other and project about 1 in. all ways. The whole stool, when finished, stands 10½ in. high, and is so strong that it will support a heavy man with safety. The block of wood to which the legs are attached should be stained to match the rustic wood; permanganate of potash solution[8] will effect this. Finally, two coats of clear varnish will give a good finish to the work.

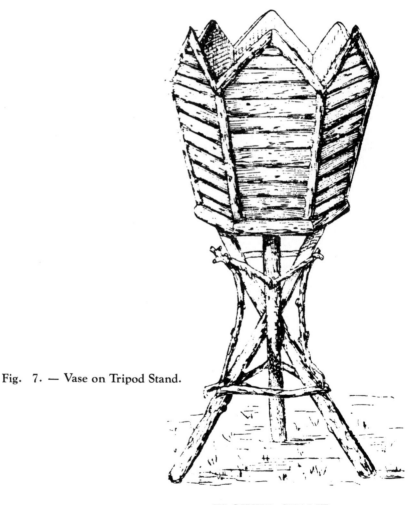

Fig. 7. — Vase on Tripod Stand.

FLOWER STAND

The flower stand shown by Fig. 7 is hexagonal in shape, with vandyked[9] sides fixed to a base supported upon tripod legs, and stands about 3 ft. 3 in. high. Elm boards are suitable for the sides and bottom; they are 1 ft. 3 in. high by 9 in. wide at the top end, and 6½ in. wide at the bottom by 1 in. thick. Shoot the edges[10] of the boards to a level of 60°, and fix them with nails driven as shown at Fig. 8. When the six sides are completed, prepare the hexagon baseboard to suit. Bore holes in it for drainage, and also bore three equidistant holes, 1¼ in. in diamter, at an angle of about 60°, for the tenons of the legs to enter (see Fig. 9). Next screw the base to the sides, and fix on the barked rustic work. The twigs for this should be seasoned at least one year before using. They are sawn in halves, straight twigs being selected for the purpose. If necessary, shoot the edges slightly, so as to obtain a closer fit when fixing them in parallel. Begin by attaching the lower border to the hexagonal base, then the upright pieces over the angles, hollowed as shown at Fig. 10; next fix the top sloping pieces, and finally the horizontal twigs. The legs are nailed at the base of the vase (see Fig. 9); and at the centre, where they cross, they are further secured with twigs which do the duty of rungs, as shown in Fig. 7.

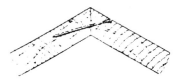

Fig. 8.
Joint of Hexagon Sides of Vase.

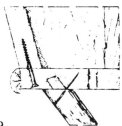

Fig. 9.
Securing Sides and Legs of Vase to Base.

Fig. 10.
Section of Twigs at Angles of Vase.

SQUARE VASE

Fig. 11 shows a square vase constructed with elm boards 1¼ in. thick. A fair size for the side will be 1 ft. 8 in. at the top and 1 ft. 5 in. at the base by 2 ft. high, including the 2½ in. plinth. The split twigs forming the decoration are 1½ in. wide, and spaced about 2 in. apart edge to edge.

Fig. 11. — Large Square Vase.

Fig. 12. — Large Hexagonal Vase.

Fig. 13. — Large Plant Vase with Claw Foot.

HEXAGONAL VASE

The vase shown in Fig. 12 is hexagonal in shape, the sides being 1 ft. 8 in. high by 1 ft. 2 in. wide at the top edge, and 1 ft. ½ in. at the base. The sides and bottom of both vases are connected as in Figs. 8 and 9. Five 1 in. holes are bored for drainage. The short feet having been secured with screws driven from the inside, the split rustic work is bradded on in the same order as that described for Fig. 7.

The stands and vases should be given two coats of oil varnish, allowing the first coat to dry before applying the second.

VASE WITH CLAW FEET

A big plant vase made from half a paraffin cask[11] is illustrated by Fig. 13. An ordinary 40 gal. cask stands, roughly, some 3 ft. high, has

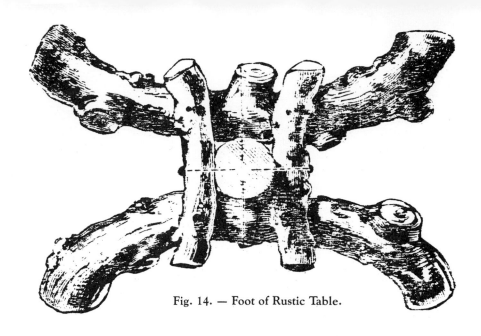

Fig. 14. — Foot of Rustic Table.

a diameter of some 2 ft., and is made of good stout oak. Sawn through the middle, the paraffin barrel makes two admirable tubs. One such half is shown in Fig. 13. That it is proposed to render suitable for some large bushy plant, so it will have to be mounted on legs. The legs shown are simply so many pieces cut from rough branches. From a heap of stuff one can generally choose pieces sufficiently adapted to the purpose though their exact contours will, of course, vary. Oak branches, technically known as "bangles," from which the bark has been taken will do well; or if the bark is liked, apple-tree or elm boughs will be suitable. That these sticks should be rough and gnarled and knotted add to their effect. As the tub will be only partly covered with rustic mosaic work, it will be well before nailing anything upon it to paint it. A good dark brown or chocolate will go well with the natural bark. The rustic pieces will have to be cut through with the saw, the lengths being too great to be safely split with the hatchet — that is, with the exception of those around the lip, which are of thicker rod than the zig-zags; say, 1½ in. as compared with 1 in. Generally speaking, brads are to be recommended for fixing rustic mosaic, but where, as in the present, the strips have to be bent over a carved surface, small nails will be found more secure. Groups of fir cones, as shown, will prettily ornament the triangular spaces.

A style of foot suitable for a one-leg flower stand or table is illustrated in plan and part by Fig. 14.

SQUARE TABLE

A small rustic table which may, if desired, be used as a flowerpot stand, is illustrated by Fig. 15. The top may be made of ¾ in. stuff, and should have two ledges (see Fig. 18) nailed underneath to

Fig. 15. — Square Table.

prevent twisting. The table may be 1 ft. 10 in. high, with the top 15 in. square, or, if a larger size is required, 2 ft. 1 in. high, with the top 18 in. square. The design is not suitable for tables of a larger size.

The legs may be secured to the top by boring holes in the ledges and driving them in. The cross bars must be firmly secured to the legs, and, for the joints, the mortise and tenon shown at Fig. 17 would be suitable. If the sticks used to form the legs are rather small, it will be better if the cross bars are kept a little higher on two of the sides, so that the mortises do not meet each other.

The top is covered with a Swiss overlay pattern, made of split sticks. The design may be set out by drawing lines from corner to corner on the top, and across the top in the centre of each side. A smaller square is then drawn in the centre of the top, with diagonals at right angles to the sides of the top. Lines drawn from the corners of the small square to the corners of the top will form a four-pointed star. The pattern should be clearly outlined with a pencil. In nailing on the sticks, those round the outer edge of the top should be put on first and mitred at the corners. Next, the outside sticks of the small square should be nailed on, then the eight pieces from the corners of the small square to the corners of the top.

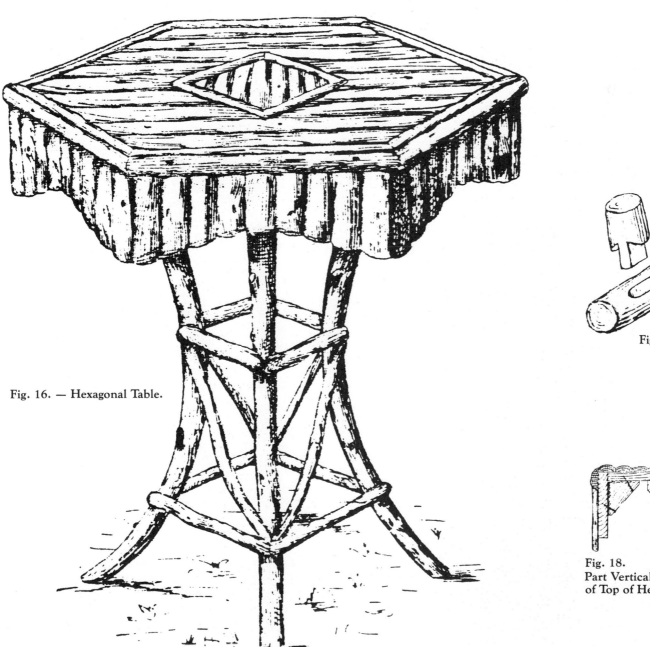

Fig. 16. — Hexagonal Table.

Fig. 17.

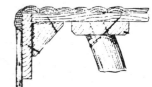

Fig. 18.
Part Vertical Section
of Top of Hexagonal Table.

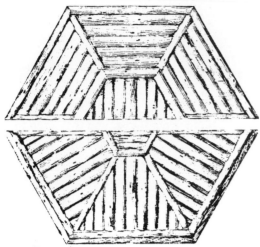

Fig. 19.
Half Plans of Top of Hexagonal Table.

Fig. 20. — Armchair.

Fig. 21.
Fixing Seat Rails
to Leg of Armchair.

Fig. 22.
Plan of Armchair Seat Frame.

In working up patterns of the above description, always nail on the sticks that follow the outline of the design first. The filling-in pieces may be put on afterwards. Variety may be given to the patterns by using sticks of different colours; for instance, the design may be outlined in hazel or blackthorn, and filled in with hawthorn or peeled willow. The edges of the table top are conceled by nailing on an edging of short sticks or cones.

HEXAGONAL TABLE

Fig. 16 shows a small hexagon-top table for use in a summer house or on the lawn. The following dimensions are suitable: Height 2 ft. 6 in., and diameter of circle for the hexagon top 2 ft. 9 in. The top is made from two or three ⅞ in. boards cramped together to the required width and fixed underneath with two battens 3½ in. wide by 1 in. thick. The four legs are dowelled and nailed to these battens and further stiffened by the rungs and the diagonal braces which are nailed to the legs. A corona[12] is fixed around the edges of the table top, and the method of securing the board is shown in Fig. 18. In Fig. 19 the half plans show two ways of ornamenting the top. The twigs should be sawn so that in section they are less than a semicircle, and it will be an advantage to shoot their edges slightly, as then they will fit closer and cover the rough boards that form the table top.

ARMCHAIR

For the armchair (Fig. 20) select four slightly curved legs about 3 in. in diameter; the front pair are 2 ft. high and the back pair are 2 ft. 9 in. high. The front seat rail is 1 ft. 2 in. long by 2½ in. in diameter, the back rail is 1 ft. long, and the side rails are 1 ft. 3 in. long, their ends being trimmed to fit the legs, and fixed with inserted ash or elm dowels ⅞ in. in diameter; see Fig. 21. The height from the ground line to the seat top is 1 ft. 4½ in. The battens forming the seat rest on the side rails, and cleats are fixed to the inner sides of the four legs (see Fig. 22) to support the extreme and front battens. The arms and back are made in three parts, the scarfed joints coming immediately over the back legs. The trellis work is then added, and finally the struts and dentils are fixed around the seat. The chair can be made from undebarked wood without any dressing, or the bark may be removed and the wood, when dry, can be finished in stain and outside varnish.

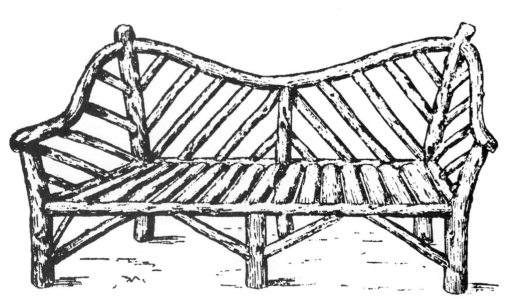

Fig. 23. — General View of Garden Seat.

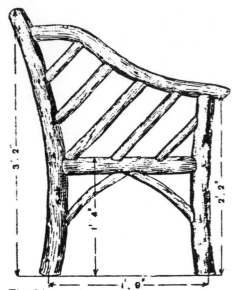

Fig. 24.
End Elevation of Garden Seat.

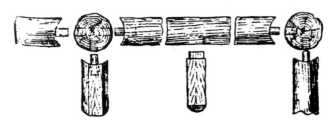

Fig. 25. — Joints of Rails and Posts for Garden Seat.

Fig. 26.
Arm-rest for Garden Seat.

GARDEN SEATS

The garden seats about to be described will look very effective if made of oak that has had the bark removed and the small twigs trimmed off clean; they should be finished in stain and varnish. In construction they are fairly simple.

For making the chair shown by Fig. 23, first select the three back posts, with their natural curves as much alike as possible. In diameter they should be from 2½ in. to 3 in. Select also two arm posts and one centre leg for the front. Next, cut two seat rails for the back and one rail for the front, 5 ft. or 6 ft. long as desired, and cut two side rails (see Fig. 24) and one centre rail, each 1 ft. 7 in. long. Work the ends of the rails to the shape of the posts as shown by Figs. 25 and 26, so

Fig. 27. — Another Garden Seat.

Fig. 28. — Cross Section of Garden Seat.

Fig. 29.
Vertical Section, Showing
Front Rail, Cross Rail, and Battens.

that they make a fairly good joint and bore the posts and rails with a ⅞ in. bit 1¼ in. deep, to receive dowels made of ash or elm[13]. These are preferable to tenons formed on the rails themselves. Now try the whole together temporarily, and make good any defects. Then take the pieces apart, and coat the joints with a thick primer. Drive the joints home and fix them with nails or screws and wipe off the surplus paint. The top back rail and the arm-rest can next be fitted. The ends of the back rail are worked bird's mouth, to fit the posts. The arm-rests are treated in the same way at the back; they fit in vees cut in the front posts, and are fixed with nails.

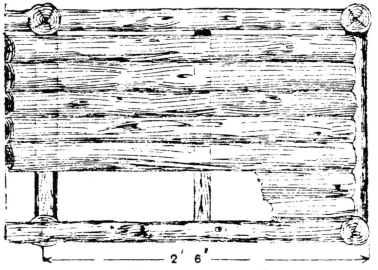

Fig. 30. — Part Plan of Seat.

Measure off and mark equal spaces for the struts, the ends of which are trimmed to fit the rails and posts. Secure them with two nails at each end. The seat is made of split saplings laid with the ends pared to fit the rails and bradded on. Finally, fit the struts between the seat rails and the lower part of the posts.

The framework for the chair shown by Figs. 27 and 28 is on the same principle as that already described. The segmental battens forming the seat run longitudinally, and their ends are shaped to fit the outer rails. The battens rest on a frame worked on the centre cross rail (see Figs. 28, 29 and 30). Fig. 29 also gives a part cross section near the centre leg, and shows the front rail placed out of centre and the cross rail resting on the leg, to which it is firmly nailed. When the seat is more that 5 ft. in length the battens require intermediate supports, which can be cut from split saplings. The panelling on the back is fixed to the top and bottom rails and supported in the centre by a wide longitudinal rail and two vertical rails at the mitres of the diamond centres. These are fitted in and

Fig. 31.

Figs. 31 and 32. — Front View and Plan of Solid Garden Gate.

Fig. 32.

secured and then the vertical split twigs are fixed partly on them and also on the rails. Finally, struts are fixed to the seat rails and legs and covered with short twigs, with their lower ends running in a regular curve.

GATES AND FENCES

In many gardens there is a space devoted to the tool house, potting shed, refuse head, etc. Shrubberies, of course, hide the unsightly appearance of this particular spot to a certain extent, but it may be found desirable to close the entrance for this part of the garden from the remainder, and the gate illustrated in front elevation by Fig. 31 is, from its semi-rustic nature, particularly suitable. Fig. 32 shows a plan and Fig. 33 is a part back view. The gate is quite simple in construction, and should be of sufficient height to obstruct the view from each side.

Local circumstances will of course determine the width of the gate, but the one illustrated by Fig. 31 is constructed on a framework 6 ft. square, the total height being 8 ft. The timber for the frame need not be planned.

Fig. 33. — Part Back View of Frame for Solid Garden Gate.

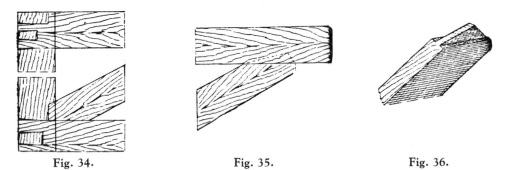

Fig. 34.   Fig. 35.   Fig. 36.

Figs. 34 to 36. — Joints in Frame of Solid Garden Gate.

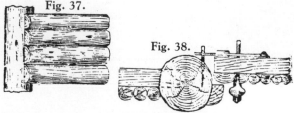

Figs. 37 and 38. — Fixing Ends of Twigs.

Fig. 39.
Detail of Closing Stile.

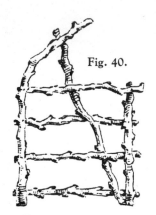

Figs. 40 and 41.
Designs for Rustic Gates.

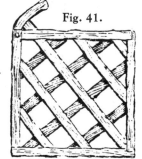

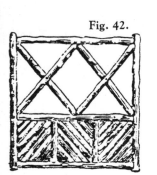

Figs. 42 and 43.
Designs for Rustic Gates.

Cut the closing and hinging stiles 6 ft. long out of stuff 6 in. wide by 2½ in. thick. The three rails are of the same dimensions and can be halved and dovetailed to the stiles, or, better, mortised, tenoned, and wedged and braced, as shown in Figs. 34, 35, and 36. Separate pieces of stuff are fixed up to the centre to form a muntin for supporting the rustic work; the necessity is obvious from Fig. 33, where it will be noticed the twigs are outlined on the frame. Each twig has a bearing on the frame, and can thus be nailed individually.

Two stout gate hinges and hooks are required, and they can be bolted on with ⁷⁄₁₆ in. bolts and nuts. Now commence fixing of the undebarked twigs, they should be as straight as possible and used in their natural shape, without being split in halves.

The terminations of the joints for circular stuff are slightly different from the ends of the half-round stuff; see Figs. 37 and 38. Start by fixing the outside squares, and finally the diagonal filling.

The posts are 9 in. or 10 in. in diameter by 9 ft. long, 3 ft. being underground. Cut three mortises in the posts to receive the rails for the side fencing. These rails are nailed flush to the secondary posts, nails also being driven through each mortise in the gate posts. Next dig the holes for the posts, these being kept at correct distances apart by nailing battens to the top and at the ground line while ramming in the posts.

A week or more should elapse before the gate is hung to the posts. This may then be propped up fair between the two posts, and the position should be marked for the staple of the latch and hooks for the hinges. A rebate is formed for the gate on the posts by nailing on split sapling; see Figs. 33 and 39. Finally, a short post can be driven in the ground and fitted with a hook for retaining the gate when open wide.

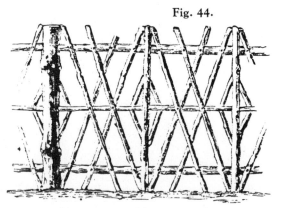

Figs. 44 and 45. — Designs for Fences.

Suitable designs for small rustic gates are given by Figs. 40 to 43. The wood for making gates to the two designs (Figs. 42 and 43) should have the bark removed. The chief rails and posts are about 2 in. thick, filled in with 1½ in. or 1 in. pieces, halved and nailed together where they cross. The joints may be hidden by bosses of planed wood (see Fig. 43). If the gate is to be removable, fix a hook on the hanging stile to engage with a staple in the joint, and a pin in the bottom to turn round in a socket. The gate is then easily taken out of its hanging. Varnish the wood on completion.

RUSTIC CARPENTRY: BUILDING YOUR OWN FURNITURE

Notes

1. Any native wood will do.

2. In England during the nineteenth century, a moderate income could be had by making the portable panels (hurdles) and stout poles (spars) used to enclose land or livestock.

3. Refers to the bottom overlay of the decorative dentils.

4. A board of fir or pine.

5. A protective edge.

6. A course tough fiber made from palms; any heavy hemp will do.

7. A tool used commonly in the nineteenth century consisting of an awl with a chiseled edge used to make holes in brads or screws. Anything such as a drill that will penetrate a coconut shell will work.

8. Any compound that will oxidize the wood, such as an oil stain, can be used.

9. During the nineteenth century, a natural brown-black pigment known as vandyke brown was made from organic matter obtained from bog earth, peat, or lignite deposits. For the purposes described here, any synthetic brown pigment will do.

10. Plane with a hard plane.

11. Any wooden barrel, such as a nail keg, will do.

12. A projecting cornice.

13. Or any other sturdy wood.

SOURCE
GUIDE

W — Wholesale Furniture Outlet

R — Furniture Retail Store

Alabama
Richard DiMarzo (R)
3113B Carousel Ct.
Hoover, AL 35216

Alaska
Hershberger's (W)
35723 Kenaceber Hwy.
Soldatna, AK 99669

Arizona
Backwoods Furniture Co. (R)
P.O. Box 1798
Cave Creek, AZ 85331

Goldwater's (R)
3100 N. Central Ave.
Phoenix, AZ 85012

Joske's (R)
18th St. and Camelback Rd.
Phoenix, AZ 85016

California
Bullock's (R)
7th and Hill St.
Los Angeles, CA 90014

John Coonen (R)
531 Cherry Ave.
Sonoma, CA 95476

Gump's (R)
250 Post Rd.
San Francisco, CA 94108

Macy's (R)
Stockton and O'Farrell Sts.
San Francisco, CA 94108

Made-in-Mendocino (R)
13500 South Hwy. 101
Hopeland, CA 95449

I. Magnin (R)
3240 Wilshire Blvd.
Los Angeles, CA 90010

My House/LA Mart (W)
1935 S. Broadway
Los Angeles, CA 90024

Colorado
The Denver (R)
16th and California Sts.
Denver, CO 80202

Joslin's (R)
16th and Curtis Sts.
Denver, CO 80202

My House/Denver Mart (W)
451 E. 58th Ave.
Denver, CO 80216

Connecticut
Wayside Furniture Shops (R)
1650 Boston Post Road
Milford, CT 06460

Bloomingdale's (R)
20 Broad St.
Stamford, CT 06901

Delaware
Besche's Furniture (W)
Georgetown Lewis Hwy.
Georgetown, DE 19947

District of Columbia
Duncan-Huggins Ltd. (W)
3311 M St., N.W.
Washington, DC 20007

Garfinkel's (R)
1401 F St., N.W.
Washington, DC 20004

Woodward & Lothrop (R)
10th and F Sts., N.W.
Washington, DC 20001

Florida
Burdine's (R)
22 E. Flagler St.
Miami, FL 33131

Jack Davidson's (W)
4 Via Parigi
Palm Beach, FL 33407

Decorator's Mart (W)
1900 S. Hickory St.
Melbourne, FL 32901

Little Tree Cyprus Co. (R)
2217 W. Washington St.
Orlando, FL 32804

Georgia
Davison's (R)
180 Peachtree St., N.W.
Atlanta, GA 30303

McCormick and Associates/
 ADAC (W)
351 Peachtree Hills Ave., N.W.
Atlanta, GA 30305

Rich's (R)
45 Broad St.
Atlanta, GA 30303

Idaho
The Bon (R)
Box 19
Boise, ID 83702

Illinois
Carson Pirie Scott & Co. (R)
One S. State St.
Chicago, IL 60603

141

Habersham Plantation Country
  Store (W)
Woodfield Mall
Schaumburg, IL 60196

Marshall Field (R)
111 N. State St.
Chicago, IL 60603

Indiana
William H. Block (R)
50 N. Illinois St.
Indianapolis, IN 42604

Hickory Furniture Works (R)
403 S. Noble St.
Shelbyville, IN 46176

Kentucky
Randy Hobson (R)
2226 Tamarack Rd.
Owensboro, KY 42301

Terry Ratliff (R)
General Delivery
Manton, KY 41648

Shillito's (R)
7900 Shelbyville Rd.
Louisville, KY 40222

Louisiana
The Custom House (W)
5425 Highland Rd.
Baton Rouge, LA 70808

Godchaux's (W)
828 Canal St.
New Orleans, LA 70112

Habersham Plantation Country
  Store (W)
9569 Courtanna Pl.
Baton Rouge, LA 70815

Maine
Day's Inc. (R)
542 Congress St.
Portland, ME 04111

Jayson Co. (R)
73 India St.
Portland, ME 04104

Maryland
Jesse Benesch & Associates (W)
6245 Falls Rd.
Baltimore, MD 21209

Hochschild Kohn & Co. (R)
200 N. Howard St.
Baltimore, MD 21201

Massachusetts
Bloomingdale's (R)
175 Boylston St.
Newton, MA 02167

International Printworks (W)
110 Gould St.
Needham, MA 02194

Jordan Marsh (R)
450 Washington St.
Boston, MA 02111

Walpole Woodworkers (R)
767 East St.
Walpole, MA 02081

Ward's Nursery (R)
Rt. 7
Great Barrington, MA 01230

Michigan
Rozmallin (W)
1700 Stutz Dr. #38
Troy, MI 48084

Minnesota
Dayton's (R)
700 Nicolet Mall
Minneapolis, MN 55402

Mississippi
Batte Furniture Co. (W)
1010 E. Northside Dr.
Jackson, MS 30206

David Moore (R)
P.O. Box 875
Rosedale, MS 38769

Missouri
Famous-Barr Co. (R)
601 Olive St.
St. Louis, MO 63101

Stix, Baer & Fuller Co. (R)
601 Washington Ave.
St. Louis, MO 63101

Montana
Dog Hair Chairs (R)
Rustic Furniture and Seat Weaving
2867 Foothill Rd.
Kalispell, MT 59901

Lar-Ken Furniture (W)
415 N. Higgins Ave.
Missoula, MT 59801

Nebraska
Younker-Kilpatrick's (R)
1900 A. 41st St.
Omaha, NE 68105

Peter Stratner; Photo by Nick De Candia

New York

Adirondack Store and Gallery (R)
Drawer 991
Lake Placid, NY 12946

American Country Store (R)
9696 Lexington Ave.
New York, NY 10021

The American Rustic Furniture Co. (R)
Box 168
Stuyvesant Falls, NY 12174

American Wing (R)
Main St.
P. O. Box 1131
Bridgehampton, NY 11932

Bloomingdale's (R)
1000 Third Ave.
New York, NY 10022

Robert Doyle (R)
P.O. Box 565
Lake Placid, NY 12946

Fabrications (R)
146 E. 56th St.
New York, NY 10022

Jerry Farrell (R)
225 W. 106th St.
New York, NY 10025

Ken Heitz (R)
Box 161, Rt. 28
Indian Lake, NY 12842

Hyland Fence Co. (R)
7400 Pittsford Victor Rd.
Victor, NY 14564

Gilbert Jaques (R)
East Hill Rd.
Keene, NY 12942

Margot Johnson (R)
American Standard Building
40 W. 40th St.
New York, NY 10018

Johnny Jupiter (R)
385 Bleecker St.
New York, NY 10014

Dan Mack; Photo by George W. Gardner

Johnny Jupiter (R)
884 Madison Ave.
New York, NY 10021

Vladimir Kagan (W)
232 E. 59th St.
New York, NY 10022

Kelter-Malcé (R)
361 Bleecker St.
New York, NY 10014

Daniel Mack (R)
225 W. 106th St.
New York, NY 10025

Macy's (R)
34th St. and Broadway
New York, NY 10001

Newel Galleries (R)
425 E. 53rd St.
New York, NY 10021

A.S. Perry, Inc. (R)
16-24 Fourteenth Ave.
Whitestone, NY 11357

E.G.H. Peter, Inc. (R)
390 Bleecker St.
New York, NY 10014

The Place for Antiques (R)
993 Second Ave.
New York, NY 10022

Pot Covers, Inc. (R)
101 W. 28th St.
New York, NY 10001

Spirit of America (R)
269 W. 4th St.
New York, NY 10014

Walter's Wicker Wonderland (R)
991 Second Ave.
New York, NY 10022

Wildwood Books and Antiques (R)
Route 28
Old Forge, NY 13420

Zona Gallery (R)
484 Broome St.
New York, NY 10013

New Jersey
Huffman-Koos Co. (R)
Rt. 4 and Main St.
N. Hackensack, NJ 07661

Kalkin, Inc. (R)
Becker Farms Rd.
W. Orange, NJ 07052

North Carolina
Added Oomph! (W)
P.O. Box 6135
High Point, NC 27262

Hutch Traver (R)
Rt. l, P.O. Box 230
Wake Forest, NC 27587

Ivey's (R)
127 N. Tryon St.
Charlotte, NC 28202

Malba and Hadges
Interior Design (W)
P.O. Box 86, Hwy. 1975
Cashiers, NC 28717

Ohio
Halle's (R)
130 S. High St.
Columbus, OH 43215

May Co. (R)
Public Sq.
Cleveland, OH 44141

Willow by Phillips (R)
P.O. Box 353
Medina, OH 44258

Oklahoma
Dillard's (R)
Woodland Hills Mall
Tulsa, OK 74135

The Natural Light (R)
P.O. Box 216
Grove, OK 74344

Oregon
Kneedler-Fauchere (W)
210 N.W. 21st St.
Portland, OR 97209

Pennsylvania
Amish Country Collection (R)
P.O. Box 5085
New Castle, PA 16105

Mary K. Darrah (R)
33 Ferry St.
New Hope, PA 18938

Davis and Wentz Hickory
 Furniture (R)
New Paris R.D.
New Paris, PA 15554

Joseph Horne Co. (R)
Pennsylvania Ave. and Stanwix St.
Pittsburgh, PA 16105

Interior of Erie (W)
12th St.
Erie, PA 16105

The Rocker Shoppe Ltd. (W)
1776 Eastern Rd.
Doylestown, PA 18901

Rosecore (W)
2400 Market St., Sp. 214
Philadelphia, PA 19103

Strawbridge and Clothier (R)
80l Market St.
Philadelphia, PA 19107

John Wanamaker (R)
13th and Market Sts.
Philadelphia, PA 19107

Tennessee
Bell Buckle Crafts (R)
Railroad Sq.
Bell Buckle, TN 37020

Goldsmith's (R)
123 S. Main St.
Memphis, TN 37095

Walton Hughes (R)
Rt. 1, P.O. Box 121A
Liberty, TN 37095

Texas
Louis Beale/WTC (W)
6300 N. Beltline
Dallas, TX 75207

The Corner Shop (W)
Decorative Center
Dallas, TX 75207

The Country Sampler (W)
127 E. Main St.
Fredericksburg, TX 78624

Foley's (R)
1110 Main St.
Houston, TX 77002

Beverly Jacomini (R)
2013 S.W. Gray
Houston, TX 77019

Knorr Furniture (W)
15 Plaza Center
Midland, TX 79701

Neiman-Marcus (R)
Ervay and Main Sts.
Dallas, TX 75201

Patio Shop (W)
2225 S. Georgia
Amarillo, TX 79109

Gilbert Jaques; Photo by Philip Lief

Mark T. Quigley; Photo by Bill Beck

Catherine Tinney (R)
P.O. Box 1065
Brady, TX 76825

Treat & Co. (R)
10001 W. Heimer
Houston, TX 77042

Vermont
David Holzapfel (R)
Rt. 9, P.O. Box 66
Marlboro, VT 05344

Brandon Antiques Center (R)
31 Franklin St.
Brandon, VT 05733

Washington
Bon Marché (R)
Third Ave. and Pine St.
Seattle, WA 98660

Wisconsin
Boston Store
331 W. Wisconsin Ave.
Milwaukee, WI 52303

Wyoming
Lodgepole Manufacturing (R)
Star Rt., Box 15
Jackson, WY 83001